D0860451

LOOKING INTO THE PAST:
PEOPLE, PLACES, AND CUSTOMS

Customs of the World

by

Thomas Bracken

390
BRA

KOUTS
MS/HS
MEDIA CENTER

Chelsea House Publishers

CHELSEA HOUSE PUBLISHERS
Editor-in-Chief Stephen Reginald
Managing Editor James D. Gallagher
Production Manager Pamela Loos
Art Director Sara Davis
Picture Editor Judy Hasday
Senior Production Editor Lisa Chippendale
Designers Takeshi Takahashi, Keith Trego

Copyright © 1998 by Chelsea House Publishers, a division
of Main Line Book Co. All rights reserved. Printed and
bound in Hong Kong.

First Printing

1 3 5 7 9 8 6 4 2

Library of Congress Cataloging-in-Publication Data

Bracken, Thomas.
Strange customs of the world / by Thomas Barcken.

p. cm. — (Looking into the past)
Includes bibliographical references and index.
Summary: Explores customs around the world, including
the bar mitzvah, the Japanese Rice Festival, and tossing the
pancake.

ISBN 0-7910-4679-6
1. Manners and customs—Juvenile literature. 2. Rites and
ceremonies—Juvenile literature. [1. Manners and customs.]
I. Title. II. Series.
GT85.B68   1997   97-30776
390—dc21   CIP
                                                    AC

CONTENTS

Culture, Customs, and Rituals

The important moments of our lives—from birth through puberty, aging, and death—are made more meaningful by culture, customs, and rituals. But what is culture? The word *culture,* broadly defined, includes the way of life of an entire society. This encompasses customs, rituals, codes of manners, dress, languages, norms of behavior, and systems of beliefs. Individuals are both acted on by and react to a culture—and so generate new cultural forms and customs.

What is custom? Custom refers to accepted social practices that separate one cultural group from another. Every culture contains basic customs, often known as rites of transition or passage. These rites, or ceremonies, occur at different stages of life, from birth to death, and are sometimes religious in nature. In all cultures of the world today, a new baby is greeted and welcomed into its family through ceremony. Some ceremonies, such as the bar mitzvah, a religious initiation for teenage Jewish boys, mark the transition from childhood to adulthood. Marriage also is usually celebrated by a ritual of some sort. Death is another rite of transition. All known cultures contain beliefs about life after death, and all observe funeral rites and mourning customs.

What is a ritual? What is a rite? These terms are used interchangeably to describe a ceremony associated with a custom. The English ritual of shaking hands in greeting, for example, has become part of that culture. The washing of one's hands could be considered a ritual which helps a person achieve an accepted level of cleanliness—a requirement of the cultural beliefs that person holds.

The books in this series, *Looking into the Past: People,*

Places, and Customs, explore many of the most interesting rituals of different cultures through time. For example, did you know that in the year A.D. 1075 William the Conqueror ordered that a "Couvre feu" bell be rung at sunset in each town and city of England, as a signal to put out all fires? Because homes were made of wood and had thatched roofs, the bell served as a precaution against house fires. Today, this custom is no longer observed as it was 900 years ago, but the modern word *curfew* derives from its practice.

Another ritual that dates from centuries long past is the Japanese Samurai Festival. This colorful celebration commemorates the feats of the ancient samurai warriors who ruled the country hundreds of years ago. Japanese citizens dress in costumes, and direct descendants of warriors wear samurai swords during the festival. The making of these swords actually is a separate religious rite in itself.

Different cultures develop different customs. For example, people of different nations have developed various interesting ways to greet each other. In China 100 years ago, the ordinary salutation was a ceremonious, but not deep, bow, with the greeting "Kin t'ien ni hao ma?" (Are you well today?). During the same era, citizens of the Indian Ocean island nation Ceylon (now called Sri Lanka) greeted each other by placing their palms together with the fingers extended. When greeting a person of higher social rank, the hands were held in front of the forehead and the head was inclined.

Some symbols and rituals rooted in ancient beliefs are common to several cultures. For example, in China, Japan, and many of the countries of the East, a tortoise is a symbol of protection from black magic, while fish have represented fertility, new life, and prosperity since the beginnings of human civilization. Other ancient fertility symbols have been incorporated into religions we still practice today, and so these ancient beliefs remain a part of our civilization. A more recent belief, the legend of Santa Claus, is the story of a kind benefactor who brings gifts to the good children of the world. This story appears in the lore of nearly every nation. Each country developed its own variation on the legend and each celebrates Santa's arrival in a different way.

New rituals are being created all the time. On April 21, 1997, for example, the cremated remains of 24 people were launched into orbit around Earth on a Pegasus rocket. Included among the group whose ashes now head toward their "final frontier" are Gene Roddenberry, creator of the television series *Star Trek,* and Timothy Leary, a countercultural icon of the 1960s. Each person's remains were placed in a separate aluminum capsule engraved with the person's name and a commemorative phrase. The remains will orbit the Earth every 90 minutes for two to ten years. When the rocket does re-enter Earth's atmosphere, it will burn up with a great burst of light. This first-time ritual could become an accepted rite of passage, a custom in our culture that would supplant the current ceremonies marking the transition between life and death.

Curiosity about different customs, rites, and rituals dates back to the mercantile Greeks of classical times. Herodotus (484–425 B.C.), known as the "Father of History," described Egyptian culture. The Roman historian Tacitus (A.D. 55–117) similarly wrote a lengthy account about the customs of the "modern" European barbarians. From the Greeks to Marco Polo, from Columbus to the Pacific voyages of Captain James Cook, cultural differences have fascinated the literate world. The books in the *Looking into the Past* series collect the most interesting customs from many cultures of the past and explain their origins, meanings, and relationship to the present day.

In the future, space travel may very well provide the impetus for new cultures, customs, and rituals, which will in turn enthrall and interest the peoples of future millennia.

Fred L. Israel
The City College of the City University of New York

CONTRIBUTORS

Senior Consulting Editor FRED L. ISRAEL is an award-winning historian. He received the Scribe's Award from the American Bar Association for his work on the Chelsea House series *The Justices of the United States Supreme Court.* A specialist in early American history, he was general editor for Chelsea's *1897 Sears Roebuck Catalog.* Dr. Israel has also worked in association with Dr. Arthur M. Schlesinger, jr. on many projects, including *The History of U.S. Presidential Elections* and *The History of U.S. Political Parties.* They are currently working together on the Chelsea House series *The World 100 Years Ago,* which looks at the traditions, customs, and cultures of many nations at the turn of the century.

THOMAS BRACKEN teaches American History at the City University of New York, and has taught at Mercy College. A former recipient of a grant from the Ford Foundation to conduct independent historical research, he created a CD-ROM to be used as a review guide in conjunction with college curriculums, and has published biographies of Theodore Roosevelt, William McKinley, and Abraham Lincoln. Mr. Bracken lives in New Jersey.

Customs of the World

We live in a world of more than five billion people. Consider the enormous diversity implied by this huge figure—differences abound in language, in dress, in physical appearance, and in fact every aspect of our lives. But as the human race prepares to celebrate a new millennium, we have become comfortable with these dissimilarities. We celebrate, rather than deplore, our diversity.

And yet we tend to assume that ours is the best, and in fact the only, way of doing things. Owing to the weakness of human nature, we regard with suspicion anything that is strange. Upon close examination, this is not a surprise. As the first communities were formed, they were characterized not by the differences of their people but rather by their commonalities. Often, for instance, they dressed in the same manner, listened to the same music, believed in similar gods, and shared the same enemies. And from these communities nations were born.

The world today is smaller than in the past, and now, more than ever, man feels the compelling need to learn more about his neighbors. There are many values to be gained by this added knowledge, such as a lessening of racial intolerance.

At first, a foreign custom may seem meaningless or incomprehensible. Soon we discover, however, that situated within its own cultural setting, a ritual is a socially significant act to those who practice it. Many of the habits and traditions discussed in this book have existed for centuries.

They represent one small part of the cultural heritage of proud and accomplished societies.

Often, when people travel to foreign countries they find that "foreigners" turn out to be quite similar to the people we know from across the town, across the street, or from across the hall. This at first may seem a bit peculiar, especially if the "stranger" is speaking in words we don't quite understand, or dressed in clothing styles that are unfamiliar. But no matter how far we travel, people are pretty much the same.

This is important to know. We live in times when the world's peace seems constantly threatened, for reasons that we can never quite understand. Perhaps if the people of the world would stop and really get to know each other the customs and rituals of various areas of the world would no longer seem so strange.

CUSTOMS OF THE WORLD

THE ALPENHORN

I n the beautiful mountains of Switzerland, the Swiss have an unusual way of calling the cows home when the shadows begin to lengthen at the end of the day. In many districts they still use the alpenhorn, an unwieldy 12-foot-long musical instrument. It consists of a hollow tube of wood around which is wound birch bark or some other tree bark. Although it can sound only a select few notes, its effect is most striking, as these notes, echoing among the peaks, make a very unusual sound. The music of the alpenhorn echoes throughout the mountains and valleys, which alerts the villagers that it is time to bring the cows home.

In some of the higher Alps, where church bells cannot be heard, the alpenhorn was used for still another purpose, which was to proclaim to the people that the vesper had arrived. Immediately after the sun set, the *Senn*, or priest, would raise his horn and chant into it the first words of the psalm "Praise ye the Lord." This is the symbol for all local residents to uncover their heads and begin their evening prayers.

The alpenhorn also played a significant part in another Swiss convention, as it was this call from one cowherder to another situated on a distant peak that led to yodeling. Through trial and error, herders were able to use different vocal tones in their calls, and by prolonging some of them they found that their voices were able to carry farther and farther. In this way, the Swiss yodel developed.

AFRICAN INITIATION CEREMONY

n Africa, the journey from adolescence to adulthood was celebrated in many ways by different tribes in the past. Among the Lebou, this was the occasion to expand formal education, and young men were required to take a one-year course of instruction in the history of the Lebou people. In the region of Kindia the occasion was celebrated quite differently. Here, young men kept up a commotion by endlessly shaking rattles which were made of pieces of gourd cut into pieces with squared edges.

In the Zie tribe, it was the women who marked the occasion through their participation in a communal dance accompanied by the music of a drum and tom-tom. Those who observed the dance stood to the side and shook a leafy branch while joining in a group chant. The percussionists who supplied the music were considered among the highest class of professionals by the Zie tribe.

In the Bayaka tribe, the occasion was sometimes not all that agreeable to the young initiate, as usually the boy was called upon to display his courage in any number of ways. He was outfitted with an eerie looking mask, similar to the one shown here, which was topped with a spear pointing toward the heavens. The young man was then marched through the village as part of an intricate ceremony allowing him to graduate into manhood.

BAR MITZVAH CEREMONY

"**T**oday I am a man!" proclaims the young Jewish boy to the members of his congregation who have gathered in the synagogue to help commemorate the occasion of his 13th birthday. Any Jewish boy who has reached this age is a *Bar Mitzvah* or, literally, a "man, or son, of duty." He is now considered old enough to fulfill the religious duties of a man and accept the full responsibility for all his actions.

A Jewish girl who has reached the same age is called a *Bat Mitzvah*, and the ceremony and accompanying party when young women reach their 13th birthday is similar.

On the Sabbath that preceded this special birthday, the young adult will already have been called to the altar to read from the Torah (a scroll on which the Hebrew Law is written). With this act, the teen announces to all that he or she is now a full participant in the spiritual life of the congregation. After the Bar Mitzvah ceremony, the rabbi usually takes the occasion to advise the young man or woman on their future. This arrival of religious adulthood is almost always followed by a festive celebration which is highlighted by music and dancing. Here, the friends and family of the new Bar or Bat Mitzvah will gather to share the joy of the event.

In many African tribes, the witch-doctor offers several kinds of professional services—not only does he prescribe medicine but he will also control the rainfall and predict the future. It is not surprising that the training process to become a witch-doctor is quite demanding, as the man (or, in some tribes, woman) can only be chosen by a deity. After this, the person selected must then undergo a long and elaborate initiation ceremony which will often culminate in a series of violent headaches in the new witch-doctor.

The most dreaded of these religious specialists is the "oath-giver" who can control a spirit to destroy those who have sworn falsely. The only way one can become an oath-giver is to have the title passed on from his or her father. Often, however, the son or daughter will refuse it, because if even a minor mistake is made, the oath-giver can be killed by the spirit he is trying to control.

In predicting the future, the witch-doctor employs many different techniques, some of which were learned during the initiation, others which the witch-doctor invented, and still others which were purchased from some of his more renowned colleagues. None of them, however, can be successful without good moral behavior on the part of both the client and the diviner. Here, a Sudanese witch-doctor is combining his power of healing with that of predicting the future. He will reach into his magical bag for a few small bones, and "read" their position after he has thrown them on the ground. From this he will determine if the patient will live or die and how the illness should be treated.

CEREMONIAL ROAD SWEEPING

n London, there are 12 major guilds, or "companies," as well as over 80 lesser ones. Some of the major companies include Grocers, Fishmongers, and Goldsmiths, and every one developed from medieval craft guilds. Some have existed for more than 1,000 years. Today, they include more than 10,000 members, and control much of the commercial wealth of London.

As rich and powerful as these groups are, however, the public only hears about them when they perform one of their archaic and picturesque ceremonies. One of these customs is held in the city every Ash Wednesday, when the Company of Stationers distributes free cakes and ale to the public at the crypt of St. Paul's Cathedral.

Another of these quaint customs is the ceremonial procession that is held every year to commemorate the installation of new Masters and Wardens of the Worshipped Company of Vintners. As the procession inches its way through the cobblestone streets of London, it is preceded by two wine porters, nattily attired in smocks and top hats, who sweep the road that the parade will march over with distinctively fashioned brooms. This road-sweeping ceremony dates back over 700 years, and the private meeting hall of the Vintners has survived such disasters as the Great Fire of 1666 as well as the German bombings during the Second World War.

GIRAFFE-NECKED WOMEN OF BURMA

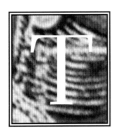

To the people of Burma the adage, "Beauty is in the eye of the beholder" was particularly meaningful. In that country, which is now called Myanmar, great attention was paid to a lady's adornment. The most remarkable ornaments of all were usually hung from the ear lobes. To create a hole large enough for the heavy earrings, the ear first had to be pierced in the traditional manner, then enlarged by gradually introducing slips of bamboo into the hole. After this, a half-smoked cigar was thrust into the ear, eventually creating a hole from which huge gold earrings nearly one full inch in diameter could hang.

Many Burmese women favored the "trembling necklace." These are little charms into which diamonds were set in such a way that it almost appeared to tremble. The woman then completely entwined this piece of jewelry around her neck so tightly that it seemed as if it were choking her.

The women of Burma wanted these necklaces to be as prominent as possible, so they tried to stretch their necks. This was a long and arduous process, which began at a very early age. Young women worked several long pieces of brass around their necks. As the young girl got older and her neck grew longer, more rings could be added. When done constantly, this gradually elongated the neck.

n Scotland, Halloween has always served as an occasion for games and amusement, and the Scots celebrate the day in a wide variety of ways. Young men with a taste for mischief-making used to make creative use of a cabbage by inserting it into the keyholes of houses belonging to people who had offended them. In another unusual Scottish Halloween custom, lovers place three dishes on the floor, one empty, one with clean water, and one with dirty water. Blindfolded, they then dip their hands into one of the three bowls. This, they believe, will determine whether the couple will marry. (Hint: Those who dip their hand into the empty dish shall remain single!)

But perhaps the most festive events of the day are the parades that take place throughout the entire country. This is a tradition which dates back more than 1,000 years. The "Druid Priest" pictured in the illustration is presiding over one of these parades. In it maidens will carry lanterns made out of turnips and dance through the streets in brightly colored costumes. Often the turnips are saved for the evening meal and mixed with chopped onions to create a dish somewhat similar to mashed potatoes. But somewhere in the bowl this meal is served in is hidden a gold ring. If your portion happens to contain the ring and you are single, you are certain to be married within the year; if you are already married, good luck will follow you for one full year—until next Halloween!

JAPANESE RICE FESTIVAL

n Japan, *Matsuri*, or festivals, are usually of sacred origin, and most relate to the cultivation of rice and the spiritual well-being of local communities. The two most common types are those which ask the gods for a successful harvest and others which offer thanksgiving in return for a good harvest. Virtually every community in Japan will offer its own version of the rice festival.

One of the interesting rice festivals is celebrated in the farming areas of central Japan, where on the evening of December 5 the male head of the household will go down to the rice paddies to welcome the chief rice deity, named *Uka no Mitama* by some communities and *Ukemochi no Kami* by others. After greeting him, the farmer will then guide the deity to the bathroom in his home, so that he might take a shower, after which the family eats a ceremonial feast before the god returns to the paddies. This rite is thought to ensure fertility to those who practice it.

Another curious version of the rice festival is the one you see pictured, where brightly colored lanterns are suspended on a long and angular bamboo pole. This pole may sometimes be as tall as fifty feet and weigh as much as one hundred and fifty pounds. The structure is thought to symbolize an ear of rice, and it is then held aloft and paraded through the streets of the community. Most of the prominent rice festivals in Japan occur in February, June, and December.

LAPP
CRADLE

n some areas of Lapland (a large region of northern Europe which includes portions of Norway, Sweden, Finland, and Russia) the sun does not rise for more than seven weeks, and because of this the people there have an old saying, "It is better to move than to stay in one place." For thousands of years, the natives of Lapland wandered the land eight months of the year, remaining in their winter encampment from Christmas to Easter.

On these long trips away from home, which the Lapps called "spring migrations," special care was given to insure the warmth and comfort of babies. The small children were tightly wrapped in reindeer skins and fastened with sealskin straps into birch wood cradles (called the *kom*). This cradle, which was shaped like a boat and has a hood at one end to protect the baby's head, was then attached to a reindeer-drawn sleigh which allowed it to glide over the icy tundra.

Quite often, the outside of the kom was covered with tanned reindeer hide, and the seams trimmed with bright red ribbons, which lent to them a very festive atmosphere. An ancient custom of hanging silver balls above the child's head was believed to ward off evil spirits.

Today, there are about 50,000 persons who are ethnically classified as Lapps. They no longer make seasonal migrations, as most make a living from farming, fishing, logging, or mining.

MAGICAL HEALING

ealers often enjoy tremendous prestige throughout tribal societies, owing in part to the large variety of services they are expected to provide. Not only are they regarded as medical specialists, but they are also expected to deal with a wide range of social problems as well, while also being viewed as religious consultant, political and legal advisor, and even marriage counselor.

The sheer variety of techniques used by these magic healers astonishes many observers. In some tribes, healing is attempted by shooting a small dart into the patient's forehead and then drawing almost a full pint of blood. Another method is to place the patient on the floor with his head resting on a pile of antelope bones, wrapping him first in red garments and then in white sheeting from head to toe, placing oil upon him, and then setting the oil on fire, which is immediately doused by the healer. In some tribes the medicine man is actually a woman, called the *Sangoma*, and she heals by performing an exorcism during which she will engage in ritualized singing, dancing, and, in some extreme cases of illness, drum beating.

In the illustration here, the healer is attempting to cure his patient by simply blowing into his ear, which he hopes will drive the illness out of the sick man's body. With exposure to modern medicine, remedies such as these have become increasingly rare in this century.

NAVAJO SAND PAINTINGS

A central theme of Navajo myths is that illness is caused by what the Native Americans define as "disharmony." To cure ills, or to bring about "harmony," was the basic purpose of the Navajo ritual of sand painting, also called dry painting. This actually was just a part (although the most essential part) of a healing ceremony which took several days.

The sand paintings themselves were usually made on the floor of the home of the sick person, and the art depicted sacred figures. The painting must be accompanied by a magical chant, performed by a special medicine man other than the artist. The actual combination of chants and paintings was determined by the singer, and it was also his responsibility to make sure that the performance was done in a ritually correct manner. When the art was finished, the singer placed his hands, moistened with herbal medicine, on top of the sand painting. The singer then placed his palms on the patient's body. This act linked the patient with the sacred figures of the painting and, the Navajo believed, assisted the healing process.

The teamwork of all the people involved—artist, chanter, various assistants, and even the patient—was a vital part of the ceremony, and without it the "harmony" sought could never be achieved.

KOUTS
MS/HS
MEDIA CENTER

New Guinea Ceremonial Costume

he first thing a visitor to a New Guinean tribal ceremony would hear are the slow, rhythmic shouts and cries of a group of men, many of whom are carrying bows and arrows. The young men have oiled their bodies until they glisten, and from their necks and waists hang long strips of shells. As the music's intensity increases, the men begin to jump up and down, and they will do this for such a long period of time that many will have to stop for a while to rest before resuming their ceremonial dance.

There are women present, but they are mere spectators who stand outside the ring of dancers—their role seems to be to provide the music (mostly drums) or carry long torches to illuminate the area. Whatever children are present are scattered randomly through the crowd, dancing with their hands stretching toward the heavens. The music quickens. Shouts of "jo-jo-jo-jo" are followed by particularly violent leaps on the part of the dancers.

This is a ceremonial costume dance of the native people of New Guinea, where dances are such an important element in their culture that they are sometimes held only in sacred houses of worship. Other dances are held on communal grounds and may be attended by several thousand people. But the occasion does not have to be sacred. Dances are held for almost any reason—for the queen's birthday, for instance, or for the opening of a new school!

PAPUAN WITCH DOCTOR

he reputation of a witch-doctor in Papua New Guinea is above reproach—the natives of this South Pacific land believe that illness is always the work of evil spirits, and if the patient dies, it is because of these evil spirits. If, however, he recovers, it is due to the great powers of the medicine man, whose reputation will then grow because he has offered visible proof of the powers he possesses. The people will rejoice, because the witch-doctor is the only one among them able to fight these evil spirits.

The remedies a medicine man relies on vary according to the particular illness he is combating. If he is fighting the *Wada*, an invisible man who can kill with just one touch of his hand, he will concoct a special mixture of rotten bananas and other ingredients to defeat him. Often, the medicine man will rely on the ritual sacrifice of a pig to overcome certain illnesses, as the blood of the slaughtered animal is spilled over magical stones and the leaves of edible ferns. This sacrifice is believed to be very pleasing to the benevolent spirits who control the healing process.

In the illustration, the witch-doctor is wearing a most unusual outfit that is an important part of the healing process, which enables him to perform the necessary dance steps in order to achieve his desired cure. Only by swaying back and forth, and then side to side, while all the time chanting a special combination of words and musical notes, will the evil spirits affecting the patient be chased away!

By all accounts, it was a most unusual event that took place in the small German town of Hamelin on the 22nd day of July, 1376. That year a great plague of rats had descended upon the town, and its citizens were not prepared to deal with them. Suddenly, there appeared among them a rather odd man, dressed in a brightly colored coat, who promised to rid the town of its problem in exchange for a certain amount of money. The fee was set, and the stranger began playing a bizarre tune with his pipe. The uncomfortably shrill sound caused every rat in the town to immediately desert its lodging and flee to the nearby Weser River, where the rats were drowned.

However, when the piper attempted to claim his money, the townspeople refused to pay him, and accused him of being a sorcerer. To exact revenge, the piper then played a tune which drew all of the town's children to a small hill just outside of Hamelin. In some stories, the children never returned home; in others, when the children did return home, all but one was lame!

Over six centuries later, this legend is still alive to the people of Hamelin—music is not allowed to be played on the streets which the piper is believed to have walked (even if a bridal procession is passing through), and the town itself dates its public documents from this calamity. Also, the strange event is still reenacted by the boys of the town, who on summer Sundays will dress themselves as rats and follow a piper on a parade outside the city.

THE RIPON HORN BLOWER

 he residents of Ripon, in the Yorkshire district of Northern England, have a rather note-worthy custom which commemorates the return from Rome of their Bishop Wilfred to the monastery he had founded. Wilfred built the monastery about A.D. 670, and because of his efforts the town of Ripon ranks as one of the three original Christian centers in all of Yorkshire.

Each night, at precisely nine o'clock, a specially made ram's horn is sounded from right in front of the mayor's house, who was called the "Wakeman," or "Watchman," in medieval society. This first sound of the horn is immediately followed by another, but only after the one blowing the horn has crossed the main square of the town and has positioned himself in front of the Market Cross. Tradition dictates that the musician must be attired in a red coat and three-cornered hat, and the horn itself must be decorated with silver badges and the insignias of trading companies with headquarters in the town. Quite often the horn that is used can last for more than one hundred years in the performance of its duties.

If you ever find yourself in this part of England and you hear a strange and unfamiliar noise at 9 p.m., it may indeed be the Ripon horn blower, as the nightly custom is still practiced to this day!

SAMOAN TATTOOING

undreds of years ago, before a Samoan boy's 11th birthday, he was called a *tamatiti* or "little boy," and during his adolescence he was referred to as a *tama*. However, it was only after passing a ritual of manhood that the youth would be permitted to join the men of the community, and this was the ultimate goal of every young Samoan boy.

The ritual included tattooing, which was an extremely painful and wearisome process, made additionally so by the group pressure involved. In traditional Samoan society, an untattooed boy could never be admitted into the *aumaga muli*, or final phase of community life. If this were to happen it would cause him much shame, as it would indicate that he had not yet attained the strength of a man to do his share of the community's work.

But the tattooing procedure is not the only element of entrance to the aumaga muli. After it the new member will present to his council of chiefs a handsome present of food, the size of which varies according to the rank of the boy. If this gift pleases the chiefs, the young boy is considered a man.

With increasing exposure to the West throughout the 20th century, far less than half the male population of Samoa still undergoes this ritual, and it is performed at a far more advanced age. No longer does it have any connection with puberty, and likewise it is no longer accompanied by cere-monies. It is now merely a matter of paying the tattoo artist.

SAMURAI SWORD MASTER

ince the eighth century, the sword has played a prominent role in Japanese society, as much for its elegant shapes and lines as for its keen edge. Throughout Japan's feudal history, the swordsmith, called the *yamabushi*, was held in high regard, and his talent was considered an art form or a magical skill by his countrymen. Student apprentices were part of a religious sect. Each morning they dressed in ceremonial costume before praying to the gods that their work would be a success.

However, during the Meiji Period (1868-1912), in an effort to modernize Japan as quickly as possible, many old customs of the country were cast aside, including the significance of the swordmaster and samurai warrior. Today, strangely enough, most of the swords from Japan's "Golden Age of Swordmaking" are found in either the United States or Europe. The ancient swords that have remained in Japan serve as family heirlooms.

Every year in Kyoto, one of Japan's most sacred cities, there is a Samurai Festival in which the people dress in colorful costumes that represent various periods in Japanese history or famed national personages. At this festival, and others like it, those families lucky enough to still possess the treasured sword will parade it through the city as part of the celebration. The Samurai Festival is part of the national Jidai Matsuri Festival, and has been commemorated since 1895.

SCORPION EATING

hroughout history, dervishes have played vital roles in the religious, social, and political life of many Islamic communities. A dervish was a Muslim mystic bound by tradition to serve his sheik, or master, and to establish a special rapport with him. In the 12th century, the main ritual practiced by the dervish was the *dhikr*, which involved the repeated utterances of a devotional phrase in praise of the Muslim god Allah. This was a very ecstatic experience for the dervish.

Rituals like this stressed the dervishes' attainment of hypnotic states and trances through not only the repeated incantation but also through such physical exertions as whirling, dancing, singing, and unusual feats or ideals unique to one particular brotherhood. It is no wonder then that, in the pursuit of their spiritual mission, dervishes were commonly referred to as "howling," "whirling," or "dancing." While they often wandered the country as teachers, their primary function was to provide loyal service to their sheik, and their devotion to this purpose knew no limits.

One example of their zealotry in this respect is found in Tunisia, a North African country bordered by Algeria, Libya, and the Mediterranean Sea. Here, the Tunisian dervish was actually known to dine on live scorpions, including their sting, which he swallowed with absolutely no hesitation at all! This most unusual of culinary habits was believed to raise the dervish to a rare level of holiness.

he *Mani-nimdu* is a Sherpa dance drama performed within the Buddhist monasteries
located in the remote hills of Tibet and Nepal. Situated in
the southern foothills of the Himalayan Mountains, this is an
area of the globe that has been practically sealed off from
foreigners until 50 years ago. The origins of this unique
variety of theater are actually extensions of mystic forms of
Buddhist worship, and they can be traced back through the
centuries to traditional Tibetan folk dance and music.

The name *Mani-nimdu* is itself derived from the name of
a sacrificial prayer chanted by Lamas (Tibetan holy men) on
various religious occasions, and the dances are performed
after the prayer as a celebration of its completion. This is
believed to bring about two desired outcomes: long life and
rain for the crops. The dance itself is performed only once a
year, but in extreme emergencies, such as a drought, the
prayers can be repeated as often as needed.

This is a colorful dance. Incense is burned, and then
amulets, magic pills, and holy water are offered to those
who have assembled to watch. They will then eat and drink
these assorted offerings and rub some of the holy water into
their heads to protect them from disease in the upcoming
months. The dancers will then appear, brightly attired in silk
costumes and masks (which are symbolic of Buddhist holy
men), and begin their sacred rite, whirling clockwise in slow
steps to the steady, cadenced sound of distant clicking, all
the while offering gifts and food to appease the gods who
are watching. The ceremonies are then followed by extended periods of prayer.

SIAMESE DANCER

I n northern Thailand (formerly called Siam), the sacred dance known as the *fon lep* has retained its traditional popularity, and is still frequently performed in many Buddhist processions and festivals. The dancers, all women, are ornately dressed in brocaded gowns, clinking anklets, and pagoda-shaped coronets. They perform their movements in a serene, slow, and highly stylized motion that suggests to the observer a sense of spiritual tranquillity and internal contemplation. Their legs are flexed, their arms outstretched, and their fingers are bent backwards in precise well-controlled movements, which together create a kaleidoscopic and almost hypnotic effect in which each movement seems to dissolve into the next.

The complex simplicity of this dance provides a direct contradiction with other dance forms of this Asian nation. Although Thailand has been opened to Western and Indian influences, many elements of the dance have remained unchanged for centuries. Tradition is so important that both the detailed movements of the dance and the music that accompanies it are dictated by Buddhist principles. Training in the symbolic postures and gestures begins during a dancer's childhood, and the performers, who are chosen at an early age, spend their entire lives attempting to master this exotic and beautiful form of expression.

SNAKE PRIEST

The Hopi Snake Dance is celebrated each year by having its participants dance with live rattlesnakes hanging from their mouths! It is a purely religious ceremony for the Native Americans who perform it. Half-naked and grotesquely painted, these natives of northern California will hang the huge diamondbacks or deadly sidewinders from their mouths as part of an elaborate series of prayers to their gods.

Their primary god is the Plumed Serpent, and through the snake dance the Hopis are asking him for the life-giving rain that will sustain their precious beans, squash, and corn crops for another year. While rattlesnakes are most commonly used, garter snakes, ball snakes, and just about any other snake they can capture can also be used. Hopis believe that all snakes are messengers to the gods and that they will both inform them that the Hopis remain obedient to the old ways, and implore them to send them their valuable rain.

This strange rite started centuries ago with the legend of *Tiyoi,* the "Snake Youth," a prominent member of Hopi mythology. As the snake dance is always held in August, which is usually the rainy season for that part of the country, it usually will rain within twenty four hours of the ceremony, and sometimes even during it. This, of course, further convinces the Hopis the snakes have been successful in their mission, and that their prayers have been answered. Incredible as it may seem, participants in the dance rarely become afflicted with poisonous snake bites!

t the end of winter, as cows are led from their cozy sheds to begin their long march to distant Alpine pastures, one of the most festive events of the Swiss year occurs. The large herds, numbering sometimes up to 200 animals, are garlanded in flowers and accompanied for much of the distance by town residents who sing and dance. The big bells you see being taken out of their winter quarters are rung in tune to the songs of the mountaineers, who warble them out with a gusto that is rarely equaled.

To one not familiar with these nature songs, the sound of these *Trychlen*, as they are called, when heard close at hand, may not be all that pleasant. This may be particularly true for the resounding tinkle of the cowbells. But as they slowly distance themselves, even by a few hundred yards, it is astonishing to hear how harmonious and pleasing to the ear the sounds become. Instead of loud and blaring noise, what the ear detects is sweet accord in which each note falls into its proper place and produces a most pleasant melody. As the chorus echoes and reechoes through the hills, it produces a most magical effect, which is often heightened by the gentle lilts of "Tra-la-la!" or "Allihoh! Allihoh!" which are soon picked up by other voices in distant fields.

These songs are often in praise of the herdsman's life, and it is claimed that if you hear their rendering once you will remember the experience for the rest of your life.

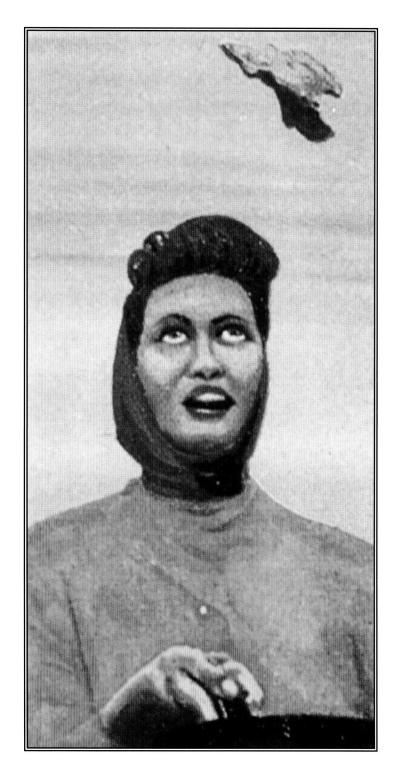

TOSSING THE PANCAKE

he association of pancakes with Shrovetide (usually the day before Ash Wednesday) is an ancient one throughout England and Scotland. For centuries, the poor families of Nottinghamshire have been provided with butter, lard, and frying pans to make their pancakes on this day, and then invited to eat them in the largest mansion in the entire town. There is only one catch: when the pancake needs turning in the pan, this can only be done by tossing it high into the air and catching it in the pan with the uncooked side downward.

When the children of Berkshire are fed their customary pancakes on this special Tuesday, all will chime:

> *Knick-knock, pan's hot,*
> *I'm come a shroving*
> *Bit of bread and bit of cheese,*
> *That's better than nothing.*
> *Last year's flour's dear,*
> *That's what makes poor Perley children*
> *come shroving here.*
> *Hip, hip, hurrah!*

On Shrove Tuesday, Westminster is the scene of an annual lemon fight. Each boy is provided half a lemon to flavor his pancake, but the lemons are never used for this purpose. Instead, they are used to engage in a fun-filled "war" with the rest of the town's inhabitants after everyone has finished eating.

But perhaps the most unusual way of commemorating Pancake Day is to be found in the town of Olney, where each year competitors run a 415-yard race while carrying a frying pan. Inside the frying pan are pancakes, and during the race each contestant must flip them at least three times. Only women are allowed to run in this race.

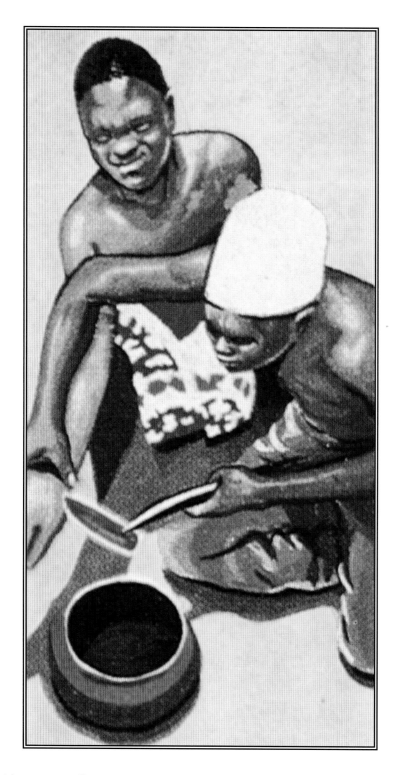

rial by ordeal" has been a common feature of justice in nearly all civilizations for thousands of years. In ancient Mesopotamia, if a man was accused of laying a spell on another he had to dive into their sacred river—if the waters of the river drowned him, the accuser was awarded the house of the dead man, but if he survived, the accuser was put to death!

In medieval England, people born with physical deformities as slight as a harelip or birthmark were often accused of witchcraft. The suspected witch, usually a woman, was then forced to endure the "Trial by Water." In this ordeal, she would be thrown into a river to see if she sank or swam. If she floated, it was deemed a sure sign of guilt. This would result in her accuser pushing her under the water with poles until she drowned.

Variations of these ordeals were also common in several tribal societies in Africa, where the "trial" consisted of such painful exercises as walking on hot coals or repeatedly immersing the head of the accused under water. In Kenya, instead of hot coals a red-hot piece of metal was used to determine guilt or innocence. The "defendant" was touched with the metal, and if it burned him he was guilty. If not, he was declared innocent and set free.

WALPURGIS MASQUERADE

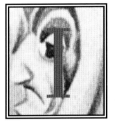

I n parts of Germany, Walpurgis Night is celebrated on April 30, the evening before the anniversary of the enshrinement of the relics of St. Walpurga. During her life, the saint governed a community of monks that had been founded by her uncle, St. Boniface. She also studied medicine and was reported to have caused miraculous cures of several very ill people who came to her in search of healing.

St. Walpurga died in about A.D. 778 and was entombed in a rock from which an eerie bituminous oil flowed. The local residents of the town soon came to believe that this oil came from the remains of the saint, and attributed extraordinary healing powers to it, calling it Walpurgis oil. A church was built on the rock, and it soon became the destination of many pilgrimages.

Legend has it that on the eve of her festival, April 30, witches gather from all over and hold a huge wild party on the very spot where the saint was buried. On this date, some residents of many German towns will dress up in attire similar to them and "battle" their more friendly neighbors. If you live in these towns, it pays to help the good spirits—those who do are believed to have good luck that will last until the next Walpurgis Night. Because the relics of St. Walpurga have been shared with several other European countries, her feast day is commemorated on different days in other countries.

A Timeline of the Beginnings of Many Customs of the World

A.D. 300   The exact origins of the Hopi tribe, and their celebration of the Snake Dance, are unknown. The Hopis are believed to be one of the oldest North American tribes, and the earliest reference to the Snake Dance dates to about this time

A.D. 670   Monastery is built in Ripon, England, by Bishop Wilfred

A.D. 778   Death of St. Walpurga

A.D.. 800   Japanese sword-masters begin crafting weapons for Samurai

A.D. 800-1000   Shintoism is established as the religion of Japan, and Rice Festivals begin to be celebrated

A.D. 1000   While anthropologists have proof of Lapp interaction with people from Russia dating to this year, it is assumed the initial migration of the Lapps occurred thousands of years prior to this. There is no indication when the use of the Lapp cradle began

A.D. 1100   Around this time, Samoans begin tattooing young men as part of their rite of passage to adulthood

A.D. **1210**   Celebration of Shrovetide, the day before Ash Wednesday, becomes common in England and Scotland

A.D. **1300**   The Alpenhorn is developed by Swiss herdsmen

A.D. **1376**   The Pied Piper draws first the rats, then the children, from the town of Hamelin

A.D. **1600**   The women of Burma begin the custom of stretching their necks to accommodate ornate jewelry

INDEX

FURTHER READING

Chaundler, Christine. *Every Man's Book of Superstitions.* New York: Philosophical Library, 1970.

Cowie, Donald. *Switzerland: The Land and the People.* South Brunswick, N.J.: A.S. Barnes, 1971.

Davidson, Basil. *African Civilization Revisited: From Antiquity to Modern Times.* Trenton, N.J.: Africa World Press, 1993.

Harper, Howard V. *Days and Customs of All Faiths.* New York: Fleet Publishing Corp., 1957.

Jerstad, Luther G. *Mani-Rimdu—Sherpa Dance Drama.* Seattle: University of Washington Press, 1969.

Ohnuki-Tierney, Emiko. *Rice as Self: Japanese Identities Through Time.* Princeton, N.J.: Princeton University Press, 1993.

Romanucci-Ross, Lola, ed. *The Anthropology of Medicine: From Culture to Method.* Westport, Conn.: Bergin & Garvey, 1997.

Thompson, E.P. *Customs in Common.* New York: New Press, 1993.